Stephen J. Golds

HALF-EMPTY DOORWAYS AND OTHER INJURIES

BY

STEPHEN J. GOLDS

Copyright © 2022 Stephen J. Golds

Cover by Cody Sexton of Anxiety Press & *A Thin Slice of Anxiety*
Interior design by Paige Johnson

www.Outcast-Press.com

(print) ISBN-13: 978-1-7379829-6-8
(e-book) ASIN: B0B9G9X88X

This a work of fiction. All characters, names, incidents, and dialogue, except for incidental references to public figures, historical events, businesses, and services are either products of the author's imagination or used in a fictitious manner not intended to refer to any living persons or to disparage any company's products or services.

"Love is a dog from Hell."

~ Charles Bukowski

"I am the beast at the end of the rope."

~ Sarah Kane

"Messy, isn't it?"

~ Richard Brautigan

Grateful acknowledgement is made to:

Outcast Press for their constant support and for publishing this collection and for giving me a shot. You guys rock!

Thank you to the friends who looked over the early drafts of this chapbook.

Barb, Scott, HLR, Seb, Paige, Natalie, Gabriel, and David.

Most of all, thank you to

YOU

the reader,

because without you, this book wouldn't exist

outside

of my

own

head.

✳✳✳

FOREWORD BY HLR

"I'm well-aware nobody reads the foreword." — Will Carver

When I began reading *Half-Empty Doorways and Other Injuries*, someone jumped in front of a train. And I don't say this presumptively—as in, statistically there's a likelihood that, indeed, the moment I began reading, someone, somewhere in the world, ended their life by launching themselves into the path of a speeding passenger train—I say this as an actuality.

It was a bitterly cold Saturday in early February. I was on the 16:33 train from London King's Cross to Leeds. Subway stations, last trains, and desolate platforms are a recurring motif throughout Golds' oeuvre, so to read his newest poetry collection while on a train seemed fitting. I'd just travelled past my home in North London and was hurtling through the Hertfordshire countryside, where Golds grew up. My Kindle lit up, *Half-Empty Doorways* loaded, my pen and notebook poised. I was ready to fully immerse myself in Golds' new verse.

The book's dedication alone made me smile, my knowing grin reflected in the darkened train window—if this collection was anything like his *Poems for Ghosts in Empty Tenement Windows I Thought I Saw Once* (Golds loves an epic title), I knew I was in for a deliciously depressing treat. I was several poems in, falling head-over-heels (again) for Golds' candor, his saying-it-like-it-is, no-fucking-about, this-was-real-and-it-hurt delivery, when our train screeched to a sudden halt. I glanced up, wondered where the fuck we were, what the holdup was, frowned at the bloke across the carriage listening to rugby on his phone without headphones (unforgivable), then returned to Golds' words.

I greedily scrolled back a few pages to the opener, to linger on the repetition of "All sleek chrome / and mean intentions," to feel the true effect of the double image, to clock the rhythm of the syllables. Because that's the thing: loving Golds' poetry as much as I do, I was so hungry to devour this whole book, almost manic, eager to absorb all of it, every poem, every image. In fact, as was usually my plan when given an ARC to write a blurb or intro for a writer I admire, I'd decided to rush through it, ravenous, as if downing a first pint to quell my shakes, and then, once I'd gotten the initial thrill out of my system, go back to savor the second reading, sipping slowly, re-reading deeply and thoughtfully, taking notes, analyzing, absorbing, dissecting (I think I've re-read Golds' First Cut collection, *Poems for Ghosts*, about 10 times in 18 months, such is the power and magnetism of his work). Then the conductor made an announcement to scupper my plans: "Ladies and gentlemen, unfortunately the train in front of us has hit a person at Stevenage. In case you missed that, a PERSON has been HIT by the TRAIN just AHEAD of us."

The carriage erupted into a chorus of "Oh, for fuck's sake"s, tutting and sighing, a little girl crying, no doubt envisioning horror in her innocent head. Two men behind me launched into ignorant complaints about how "selfish" suicide was. One said, "Why couldn't the guy just hang himself at home init, 'stead of fucking up everyone's day?" I flinched, feeling a little sick, recalling "Unbalanced," Golds' poem that will haunt me for as long or short as I live: "When I was 8 years old / I tried to hang myself / from my cabin bed / with a belt // because all of / my broken toys / wouldn't fit / in the toy box. // When I was 34, / I tried again / for the same / reasons."

The driver told us to expect severe delays. "In my experience," he said, "the fastest time this issue has been... resolved in the past, is 45 minutes, but it usually takes at least three hours for the British Transport Police to establish the facts and clear the tracks." I almost admired the poetry of it, wondered if he'd rehearsed this speech at home, then I realized he's probably had to say this spiel too many times throughout his career. "Unfortunately, we can't go around it. So, sit tight, girls and boys. We're going to be here for a while." Cue more complaining, more vitriol directed towards the dead person who just inconvenienced us all by ending their suffering. I was travelling alone and, facing the prospect of a long evening stuck on a freezing LNER just outside of Knebworth with only one cigarette left, had never been gladder to have Golds' words as company, for however many hours I would be stuck on this train full of angry people, feeling "Alone in an occupied room."

The incident rattled me for many reasons: Obviously, it was terribly sad, but then, I got to a poem titled, "The 7:51 Train Has Been Delayed," where Golds effectively summarized the suicide I'd just been affected by in words I didn't have: "A whole life, desperately, isolated – / extinguished into a simple inconvenient incident. / I couldn't help / but feel that a point / had been proven / somewhere. Somehow." I was completely thrown by this coincidence.

Maybe it was the palpable feeling of haunting and being haunted that pervaded his collection—all of the ghosts and shadows that traveled throughout the text ("well-aware these nights are full of / starving ghosts — hungry / for all the things we were and / all the things we will never be."), the frequent appearance of liminal spaces ("The most painful things in life / happen to us / when we are / standing within the frames / of / half-empty / doorways."), Golds' conjuring of his past loves and selves, the notion that all of us were walking an endless tightrope, perpetually teetering over life and death—that made everything feel a hell of a lot eerier. But I also think it was all the more jarring because, as you'll discover when reading Golds' *Poems for Ghosts, Half-Empty Doorways, Love Like Bleeding Out*, or any of my poetry, Golds and I have been in the same desperate frame of mind as the person who, just moments ago, deliberately met their end in such a violent manner...

On the train, I bought an overpriced Twix bar, blocked out the bitching and grumbling of my fellow passengers, and let the gravity of Golds' truths sink into me. When I finally left the train, four hours later, I was a different person than who boarded it.

    This collection was everything I wanted: an accomplished portfolio of brutal brilliance, each poem classically Golds, every word entirely true to himself. When I first read the lines, "I try to write down / the words for her that would / catch at the breath, / snatch at the hearts and / jab at the minds of all those / who read them," I thought, *Well, I don't know about her, but you've certainly done that for me*. It's hard to pick a favorite poem, as each verse holds its own, each has its own impact and strengths, but "Antiseptic Cream" is one of the best Golds has ever written (and is proof of why the "40 lines and under" preference in poetry needs to get in the bin).

    You'll find all of the things we've come to love and expect from Golds' poetry—recurring themes and images of brokenness and emptiness, ferociously honest self-examination (particularly in the poems "What We Talk About When We Talk About Anything," "I Am," "Laugh Now, Cry Later," and "This is What It All Burned Down To"), and lines that you're tempted to get tattooed ("'Death is a subtle sound / screaming to be heard.")—but you'll also be glad to learn that life isn't all bad.

    It's not all empty whiskey glasses and delayed trains and mental illness and unsurvivable heartbreak and pain in its myriad of savage forms. You'll learn that life is love. Yes, there will always be those mad loves, those all-consuming loves, those destructive, dangerous, car-crash loves, the type of love that can push a person to their death, but, in this world, there also exists love in its purest, stripped-down, most gorgeous, important form: the type of love you'll read about in the poem "For M & N II," the type of love that can save a person's life over and over and over again. And that's the love we all need to cling onto if we are to survive this cruel world.

TABLE OF CONTENTS

For Y	Pg. 13
Tu et Ego	Pg. 15
Costs of Some Things	Pg. 16
Jane Doe	Pg. 18
Leaving Home for Work with OCD	Pg. 19
C Major	Pg. 24
Collect the Reward for the Crime You Helped Commit	Pg. 25
Scattered on the Ground	Pg. 26
Please Hold. Your Call is Important to Us	Pg. 27
Staring into an Empty Whiskey Tumbler in an Empty Bar Again	Pg. 30
Often, I've noticed	Pg. 31
Perpetual Motion	Pg. 32
It's Friday and I'm Dying But It's Okay	Pg. 33
Love Hotel in My Old Hometown	Pg. 34

CONTINUED CONTENTS

Beach Girl Blues	Pg. 35
This is What It All Burned Down To	Pg. 36
Please Forgive Me, But	Pg. 37
Antiseptic Cream	Pg. 38
December and	Pg. 43
I Left You on Route Regret	Pg. 44
A Flashing Blur of Faces And White Noise	Pg. 45
Requiem	Pg. 46
Sometime Early Saturday Morning	Pg. 47
Sadie, My Love	Pg. 48
The 7:51 Train Has Been Delayed	Pg. 50
The Place You Used to Work	Pg. 51
Scared	Pg. 52
I Am	Pg. 53
Toxic	Pg. 54

CONTENTS CONTINUED

Old Movies about Poltergeists	Pg. 55
Everyone Leaves You for Dead in the End	Pg. 57
Leftovers	Pg. 59
Small-Town Crimes	Pg. 60
Alone in the Apartment With Silence Crouched Like a Pit Bull	Pg. 61
"Who Drove You Home Last Night?"	Pg. 62
Obligated	Pg. 63
Untitled #444	Pg. 64
What We Talk About When We Talk About Anything	Pg. 65
Her Name was Jenny M	Pg. 67
For M & N II	Pg. 69
Laugh Now, Cry Later	Pg. 70
Sometimes	Pg. 71
Breeze	Pg. 72
The Best Ones Are The Crazy Ones	Pg. 73

12 | Doorways & Other Injuries

FOR Y

As I was leaving
her apartment one afternoon,
she took me by the hand and led me around
her building to the garage.
Showed me the motorbike
underneath a blue tarp there.
All sleek chrome
and mean intentions.

I was surprised.
She didn't look the type.
She worked in an office and was a
saleswoman of some kind.
Medical equipment, I think.
She seemed so damn proud and
looked something else
draped over the handlebars,
smiling that pink-lipped smile,
hair hanging down.

I really liked the idea that I was fucking
a girl who rode a motorbike.
But she never rode it once
while we were together. I didn't know why.
She was one of the kindest
I had at that time.
Better than I deserved or needed.
We found each other in a dark place,
searching for a little bit of light,
promising we were just using each other
to forget about the one before.

Six months later, when I left her
for the one who almost killed me,
she cried hysterically and
I was surprised again.
She didn't look the type.

I saw her once, a few months after,
riding past me on that motorbike.
All sleek chrome and
mean intentions.
She still seemed proud and was
still something else.

I held up my hand
in an apologetic kind of wave.
She gunned the throttle and was lost to me
in the night city traffic.
I liked to tell myself that she didn't see me,
but I know much better by now.

TU ET EGO

I, I am
the garbage bag
split in the bottom,
you carry on Tuesday mornings.
The dead potted plant,
you glance at occasionally
when it's raining outside.
The radio with no batteries
on the shelf above the kitchen sink,
you'll one day place in a cardboard box
for GoodWill.

And you, you are
the twisting echo
in a smudged plate-glass window.
As all murmured reflections,
a beautiful deceit in reverse.
A sparrow in yellowed grass
for the tomcat with ripped ear and
all-encroaching darkness.
Sunlight ricocheting through
curtains the color of
torn bridal wear.

And we, we are
neither
here nor there and
what dreams may come.

COSTS OF SOME THINGS

The parents wept,
holding her small form just born.
Camera flash smiles,
blowing candles out on birthday cakes.
Wishes, meaning everything then forgotten with time.
Band-Aids, worn with pride on scraped knees.
A first pet mourned while listening to a first CD.
Losing her virginity awkwardly
in the backseat of a Toyota Corolla.

This morning... she pulled open curtains,
frowning out across a too-blue sky and sunlit rooftops.
Made a bed, shaking out the sheets.
Ate breakfast slowly while listening to the news on the TV.
Laid out clothes, wondering what was best to wear.
Did the colors clash?
Brushing her long, dark hair and then her teeth in a
cracked bathroom mirror.
Chewing at her bottom lip, arms hugged too tightly to her chest,
standing alone on a crowded subway platform on her way

downtown... she spits, gags, spits again.
On scraped knees, dabbing at smudged lips
with tissues from the small,
crumpled packet in her purse.

She passes me one, exchanging it for the cash in my
fingertips.
I tell her to take care of herself and she nods,

well aware these nights are full of
starving ghosts — hungry
for all the things we were and
all the things we will never be.

JANE DOE

They found her off the Redwood Highway. Oregon.
Pink- and beige-checkered coat rotted through.
Size 8 and a half
tennis shoes.
One braided ring with a mother of pearl stone and
38 cents in loose change.
A map of California recreational sites in her purse.
Strangled with a belt that wasn't hers and
dumped so far away
from where she was going.
Where she wanted to be.
All that remained of her,
so little not stolen.

LEAVING HOME FOR WORK WITH OCD

Okay, I've got my bag.
I've got my wallet.
Check.
Subway pass?
Check.
Wallet.
Subway pass.
Touched them?
Yes.
Yes.
In my pockets. They're there.
Okay, keys. Yes. Keys. Got them.

What about the windows?
They're closed.
Checked?
No, but I know they're closed.
Okay. Go and check them again.
Touch the glass. Touch the handles.
Yes, closed. Securely closed.
Touch them. Make sure.
1.
2.
3.
4.
5.
6.
7.

Seven touches mean they're shut securely.
Lucky seven. Lucky seven. Lucky seven.
Windows are securely closed.

Okay, gas cooker.
It's off.
Touch it, make sure.
It's cold to the touch.
Touch it seven times.
1, 2, 3, 4, 5, 6, 7.
Lucky seven.
Is it leaking gas?
I can't smell any gas.

Ignite your cigarette lighter over the grill. Make sure.
Fuck, I almost forgot my cigarettes and lighter. Okay. Got them. They're in my jacket pocket.
Touch them.
Check. They're there.
Try the gas cooker.
Yes, okay. No explosion. I'm still here. No leaky gas.
Touch the valve. Make sure it's off.
1, 2, 3, 4, 5, 6, 7. Lucky seven. Gas stove is safe.

Go and touch the windows again.
No, they're securely closed. I did the lucky seven count.
Go and check them again. Touch the glass again. Touch the handles again.
Yes, closed. Securely closed.
Touch them. Make sure.
1.
2.
3.
4.
5.
6.
7.

Okay. Fuck! Going to be late to work.
Front door.
Bag in right hand.
No, change it. Left hand. Bag in left hand.
That's better. Okay.
Wallet? Yes.
Touch it.
It's in my pocket.
Subway pass?
Yes.
Touch it.
It's in my pocket.
Cigarettes and lighter?
Yes. I've got them.
Touch. Touch. Touch. Touch. Touch. Touch. Touch.
Yes, in my jacket pocket.

What about the refrigerator? It might be open.
Fuck!
Quickly go back and touch it.
Okay, refrigerator, it's closed.
Touch it.
1, 2, 3, 4, 5, 6, 7. Lucky seven. Lucky seven. It's closed securely.
Front door again.
Keys.
Are the lights off?
Yes!
Keys.
In my hand.
Open the door and leave. Okay.
Lock the door. Check the handle.
Yes, it's locked.
Check it.
It's locked.

Check.
It's locked. Locked. Locked.
Locked. Locked. Locked.
Locked.
Fuck, going to miss the train again.
Check the door again.
1.
2.
3.
4.
5.
6.
7.
Lucky seven. Door is locked. Let's go.
Go back, check again.
1.
2.
3.
4.
5.
6.
7.
Lucky seven. Lucky seven. Lucky. Seven. Lucky fucking seven. It's fucking locked. Let's fucking go.
It might still be open. Check it again, just in case.
Fuck!
Touch it.
1, 2, 3, 4, 5, 6, 7.
Okay! Lucky seven. It's locked. Calm down. Let's go. I did the lucky seven count. Lucky fucking seven. It's good. It's locked.

Almost at the subway station.
I can make it with five minutes to spare.
     What about the front door?
It was fucking locked. I fucking checked it.

Go back make sure.
Do the lucky seven count three more times.
Just to be sure. Need to be sure.
    Fuck!
    1, 2, 3, 4, 5, 6, 7.
1.
2.
3.
4.
5.
6.
7.
1, 2, 3, 4, 5, 6, 7.

C MAJOR

No matter
all the women
I lay down in
the place
you slept,
it still remains
the place
you slept.

COLLEC THE REWARD FOR THE CRIME YOU HELPED COMMIT

Alone in an occupied room
with walls scorched black, charcoal-written letters
unsent.
The heart of the matter —
a self-immolating arsonist
begging her to
burn me up with
a late summer glance left
lingering like a
last gasoline chance
on an empty highway to
Nowhere.

SCATTERED ON THE GROUND

Taking the garbage out
this morning;
the bag split —
spilling dirty, used,
wasted things
across the broken concrete.

Reminding me of you,
and everything
you meant
to me
then.

PLEASE HOLD. YOUR CALL IS IMPORTANT TO US.

Here I am,
I'm here again.
In this place, I return,
time and time again.

The rack I've made for myself
with the brittle bones of all those, I have loved half-heartedly or half-madly.
Constructing the beams for listless, impatient gallows and
the mute crowd of bored, restless onlookers here in the audience tonight.

I'll leave when masochism finally
injures more than these
derelict rooms, rotten hardwood floors and
all the bare doorways swung wide-open here in this town tonight.

Transience. She told me,
all of us are transient. None of it matters.
Inconsequential. Catching me by surprise, like
the stray cat howling in the yard here outside my window tonight.

Supposedly perpetual. Promised,
but another candle snuffed out.
Here in the embrace of another
hungry darkness tonight.

Here I am,
I'm here again.
In this place, I return,
time and time again.

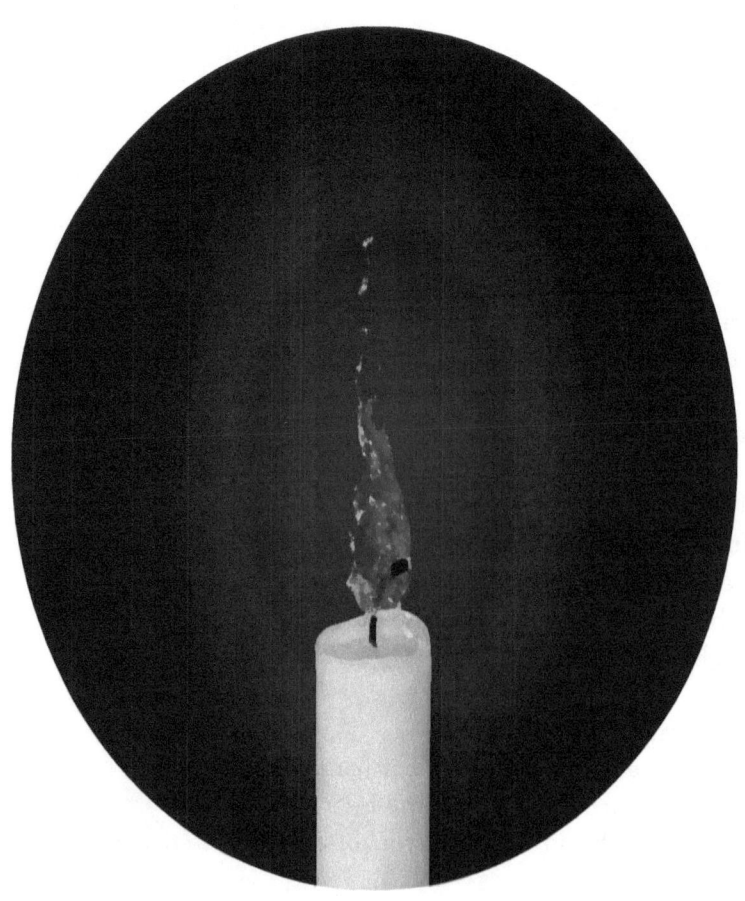

STARING INTO AN EMPTY WHISKEY TUMBLER IN AN EMPTY BAR AGAIN

I try to write down
the words for her that would
catch at the breath,
snatch at the hearts and
jab at the minds of all those
who read them.

I convinced myself they'd know her
as I knew her and they'd realize
what it was about her
that compelled me
to want to attempt
writing down anything at all.

But the words refuse to be written.
She isn't here anymore, and
writing this is as good a eulogy
as she or any reader
are going to get it now.

I know I should spend my time
pursuing things more positive, more productive,
but knowing and doing are
two very separate
things.

Besides, I'm in an empty bar,
staring into an empty whiskey tumbler.
What else is there to do
but ruminate on those things that
cannot be changed?

OFTEN, I'VE NOTICED

The most painful things in life
happen to us
when we are
standing within the frames
of
half-empty
doorways.

PERPETUAL MOTION

Over the line,
you tell me you're
coming over.
I hold the phone the way
I hold my tongue.

The way we use
each other up like kitchen
bleach
to cover the stains of
ourselves is always fun.

But it's the silence of
the apartment after,
the bed seemingly
become too small,

the smell of your
perfume –
a hangover. Talking like
strangers
awkwardly sitting next
to each other
on a long bus ride.

I know the mole on the
inside of your thigh,
but not your sister's
name,
or your happiest memory
or
anything that might
matter.

You're already damaged
it seems,
so there's not much for
me to do
with you except use you
the way you're using me.

And maybe that's okay.
I tell you to come over.
Holding the phone in my
hand
like it's a heartbreak in
motion.

IT'S FRIDAY AND I'M DYING, BUT IT'S OKAY

She said,
I was always
wrapped-up
in my own fucking head.

I said,
I'd rather be in hers
and fucking in her bed.

Leaving while she slept
and,
If I died before she woke,
I wanted her to know
she gave me something
before

we made each other
ghosts.

A fever in the night,
A house fire —
dead ashes in disarrayed,
charred remains.
She gave me something.

The only thing
she didn't take away
when
she gave me herself and
I gave her away.

LOVE HOTEL IN MY HOMETOWN

Things went wrong.
I was a married man.
Dim lights reflected on lipstick-colored mouth. Apple red.
Unknown sliding into known.
Drinks mixed with the tongue of another.

Things went wrong.
I was a married man.
Easy lies carried on currents of perfumed smoke.
Gold-hoop earrings and wedding rings on discount motel bedside tables.
Cellphones dead, killed to the outside world.

Things went wrong.
I was a married man.
What was owned was leased.
Abandoned showtime show-homes.
A stranger in my native land.

Things went wrong
I was a married man
No home, no ring, no love, no chance and gone.
Left me bleeding out,
she got away cleaner than most.
I could almost hate her for that.

BEACH GIRL BLUES

She laughed a lot.
That short, brittle kind of nervous laughter of one who has suffered constantly and needlessly. She reminded me of a dog in a pound.

One of the beautiful ones that have been
thrown away because the owners
couldn't love something more than they loved themselves.

We were both sick and I often wondered
how all the damaged and wounded ones found me
or if it was I who found them.

When she told me she worked in Soap Land selling Happy Endings, I wasn't really surprised.
I simply asked why she'd do that if she had a master's degree in psychology.
She didn't answer and I didn't ask her any more questions like that.

When we said our goodbyes, if you could call it that,
she was still laughing that same laugh and
I was relieved I wouldn't have to hear that sad sound anymore.

I do sometimes think about her and again wonder if
she found the person who could fix her
in all the ways I couldn't or just wouldn't.

This is What it All Burned Down To

38 years of
well-executed facial expressions, well-hidden sweaty palms.
Running for buses, subway trains, and bill payments.
Spoken and forgotten psalms,
orgasms with lovers loved, unloved, and misplaced.

38 years of
brushed teeth, showers, baths, shits, pisses, and moans.
Books read, unread, written, unwritten.
Words said, unsaid, should've said, shouldn't have said.
Cuts, scrapes, bruises, broken teeth, chipped teeth, and all those fractured bones.

38 years of
lights on, blown and switched off. Empty rooms, crowded rooms, and rooms I was uninvited.
Burnt toast, spoiled dinners, and napkins rolled in fingertips. Drinking until blackout, mixing drinks with meds, drinking because there was nothing else to do.
Smoked cigarettes, unsmoked cigarettes. Broken lighters. Lucky cigarettes, candy cigarettes, and cigar bars I never liked the atmosphere of.

38 years of
burning down to a noose
around the throat and
the dark hood I placed over

my own head.
Please Forgive me, but,
Your love with a bullet,
it made me a fucking cripple,
limping and hobbling
my way through life.

I pull the trigger first now.
One to the back of the head,
before they even realize
I was never really there.

Shoot first or die first is what
it all boils down to at the bottom of the glass,
when we really think about it.
If we think of it at all.

ANTISEPTIC CREAM

My girlfriend likes it
when I bite her back
when we fuck.

I let her bite me too.
Maybe, I enjoy it,
I'm not sure. It's mostly so
I don't feel misogynistic after I've cum and
we're lying in silence,
listening to the kids
in the apartment upstairs
fighting.

Sometimes, after,
when there aren't any words left,
because we've used up all our credit
in conversation for the day,
and we're looking at each other, I'm in awe.
In awe of this life.

The speed at which it moves.
One day, we were simply strangers
in a hospital elevator and
now we're naked and
she has my bite marks on her shoulders and
little pieces of my broken heart inside her that
could possibly make a child,
but won't because she's on the contraceptive pill.

Everything in life escalates.
Level by level,

all the way to the penthouse
before it plummets back down to earth
like a North Korean missile.

Then she's asleep.
I lie there with my eyes and mouth agape
in the night, listening to her breathing.
Sounds like the ocean in April,
when I swam far out and realized
I could still touch the bottom.
Made me wonder if you ever really got what you paid for.

I don't have any curtains.
The moon lights up my room like a radioactive
bottle of milk held in the hand of a geriatric patient.
I lie there unable to sleep sometimes,
dissecting our relationship,
rewinding it unkindly like a Blockbuster video
I'm taking back to the store a day late.
I won't pay the fine.
I'll just make another "new members" card with
laminated lies that will ultimately cost me more than the
fine would have.

I see us, me and her,
moving in reverse.
It's a beautiful kind of dance.
A tango that starts the way it
always has to end.
Standing alone somewhere
without change for the subway,
thinking you should've done something different but
didn't.

I sit up,
pushing the covers down,

and rub antiseptic cream into the deep scratches on my
back.
I don't have the heart to tell her that I don't enjoy that
as much as I used to.
When the claw marks are healing,
they're as itchy as hell and,
because they're on my back,
it's difficult to get the leverage to relieve
that irritation.

I think I might really feel something for this one though,
so hold that
irritation in the small, nicotine-stained space behind the
back of my lower teeth.
Rolling it under my tongue.
I see her cheeks moving too, as she slides around her own
small irritations from one side of her mouth to the other
like
 a bitter, little breath-mint of dissatisfaction.

I read on the internet that couples who share strife and
troubles with one another
live long and prosper together.

I cried in front of an ex-girlfriend once and
she fucked her diving instructor a couple weeks later.
I loved that one.
She almost killed me.
She aborted my child after we'd already talked about the
gender of it.
Given him a name.
If I believed in Hell,
I'd feel as though I had a non-refundable ticket for the
train.
I'll never make that mistake again.

Showing my guts and
stained bones.
Saying the words,
"I love you"
has always been
a game of Russian Roulette.

So, the irritations, like the insecurities and tears, stay
locked up on a chain
in an overgrown backyard.
In charcoal, I've drawn on a piece of cardboard and stuck it
at the bottom of my shoes to stop the rain
from getting in.
The rain still gets in.
I guess it always will.

And yes,
they do kill horses
kinder.
Don't they?

Tired of this dancing competition. There's no Cadillac to
win here.
I wonder if she's exhausted as I am with it all.
We can't tango together, but we can tread water and
maybe that's enough.
I'd like it to be enough.

I'll buy some new curtains from the mall and ask her to
rub cream on my back in the morning.
Maybe, she'll get the hint and maybe she won't.
That's okay too.

I want this one
to ride this rocket with me
right on down to the basement floor, exploding

into the foundations
of something I'll snap my eyes open to,
waking up with the Spring sun orange, like the tip of a
Cuban cigar
coming through my rain-stained window,
like a dog unchained, grinning with a bone in its mouth.

I'll ask her
to scratch my back, to
relieve the small irritations
not being alone so very often causes.

DECEMBER AND

It's snowing outside
my window and you're dead.
In the ground miles away.
This is where all love goes.
Into the cold earth.
And the ones who lingered,
I helped along with a pillow to the face
or revolver to the head.
Knife to the heart or unkind word.

Cleaning up the mess that stains
the floorboards and remains on my skin
with bleach and tarpaulin sheets, I always wish
to take my actions back. All the words, too.
Knowing my blood runs too hot and then too cold.

But you're dead and
it's snowing outside
my window.
It's snowing.

I LEFT YOU BEHIND ON

ROUTE REGRET

replacing you, not forgetting you,
when the door closes again,
I'm left alone with myself and
these stains of you.
Holding everything
in these palsied, arthritic hands
I'd truck with the devil for just
another moment to be with you.

A Flashing Blur of Faces and White Noise

I snap
my head up,
realizing
I missed my subway stop.
Five stops back.

I ride the train
all the way to
the end of the line
because I also realize
I've got nowhere else to be.

REQUIEM

With all the doors locked,
the curtains drawn.
The television on mute,
the clocks wound down.

I thought
I saw myself,
a ghost
in this apartment.

A broken reflection
in a grimy windowpane with
your name etched
in the dirt as I slowly rot.

SOMETIME EARLY SATURDAY MORNING

Resurfacing in a hospital bed,
being held down
by blank faces in white coats.

Naked in diaper & tube in prick.
Vomit medicinal-stench.
Stomach pumped & knowing,

knowing you haven't got the heart to change.
Holding out your hand for the nurse,
Momentarily, she's your lover or your mother.

She cringes away from you the same way you did
the dying dog you found at the side of the freeway.
Fingertips over soft, white cotton. And then gone.

Eyes rolling in skull —
Chipped stress balls, bells chiming on the inside,
belongings of
an afternoon shadow,
a madman,
alone in a hospital cot with a
television playing melancholic somewhere.
A nobody and a
never was.

SADIE, MY LOVE

I hacked another piece of myself away. Feeding it through your lips and teeth like a blender.
I was told that was what love was.

The first four fingers on my left hand,
thumb,
index,
middle,
ring
but smooth stubs.
Made giving you everything difficult.
The pinky still unhealed, gangrene and bleeding.
I persevered.
I was told that was what love was.

You smiled and licked your lips.
Kissed me once, on the scars of where my own lips used to be.
You were still so hungry.
I pressed the nub of where my right hand had been against your face as
you moved further away again.
My ankles, sawn jagged, the phantom limbs of my feet, forced me onto my knees,
to crawl closer to you and still you were hungry, Darling.
I crawled across the broken bones of what was once myself.
I was told that was what love was.

I wished to speak your name,
my tongue lived in exile at the pit of your stomach,

but you sang for me.
You sang your name in every language you knew.
The melody too loud for the holes either side of my flayed and scalped skull.
Your voice was a thousand moths with razor blade wings within my brain.
Bringing tears to my eyes, you licked away.
I was told that was what love was.

You were famished, weren't you?
You dragged my flailing torso out into the town square.
The dregs of myself that stubbornly remained.
The guillotine you had made with the promise of
your own body, the vow of living inside you, awaited me.
The sun in the late afternoon sky a nuclear blast.
The sunlight much too illuminating for a face with no eyelids.
Irises burnt away like smiles in a discolored, faded photograph.
The last lingering thought, after you collected my head, you'd find my chest empty.
My diseased, bitter heart being the first thing I gave you to swallow.
I was told that was what love was.

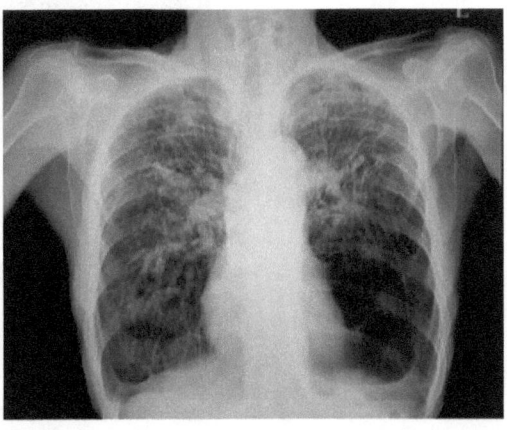

The 7:51 Train Has Been Delayed

People bitched and moaned,
glancing and frowning again at their wristwatches,
sighing into their cellphones, creating their rehearsed
disgusted faces
while shaking their vacuous skulls full of meeting times,
bill payments, net shopping,
and video games.

A rusty speaker splashed with pigeon shit, mumbling
there had been an incident,
apologizing for the inconvenience.
Someone had jumped further down the line.

A whole life, desperately, isolated –
extinguished into a simple, inconvenient incident.
I couldn't help
but feel that a point
had been proven
somewhere. Somehow.

The Place You Used To Work

Summertime, walking late, laughing, talking all night with you.

Streetlamps, lanterns, late bars, night beaches, taxi rides with you.

Fucking in the park, cheap motels, parking lots, rooftops with you.

Fighting on stairwells, driveways, airports, doorways with you.

It's summertime again and I just saw something that reminded me of you.

Got me thinking about you.

What happened to you?

SCARED

Walking a tightrope,
Swimming with sharks
Stuttering public speaking,
Swallowing hard candy

Seeing in technicolor,
Tongue-tied,
Clarity of a bleeding mind,
All my truths are in all my lies

Placing this rotten burden on
your shoulders and calling it
my love

I AM

a mutt, a special-ed freak, killer of butterflies,
devil-made-me-do-it spree killer.

A breaker of burning hearts, selfish self-harmer.
Rapist of words, singer of propaganda.

Degenerate drinker, pocket-change gambler.
One-night lousy lay, smirking deceiver.

Mentally self-inflicted, fucker of misery,
STD-spreader, eater of filth.

Intoxicated poisoner, deranged deserter,
waste of time, kamikaze lover.

I'll bury you.
I am
a collector of bones &
memento mori

Toxic
ft. BF Jones

The cowardly smoke
of a weak yet never-ending
dumpster fire,
rising slowly around me.
Stinging my eyes and
choking my words with
millions of acrid
dust particles.
Here
knowing
the only things that celebrate the dead are
crowds and crows.
Slumped picking at myself
in moldy green hallways of broken mirrors.
Places where smudged,
stained glass faces reflect shadows
that will never leave.
Here
knowing
they, like all things,
were never really here.

OLD MOVIES ABOUT POLTERGEISTS

Told me I was only seeing afternoon shadows
dancing around your halls.
Simply squirrels in your attic. No one
cooking in your kitchen.
Only dreams in your bed. Things moved but not.

Had someone in your home before
you'd slammed the door on me.
Lamps lit bright all down the avenues.
Hearing the lock *click* shut, there,
written in your words, quickly scribbled in your eyes.

What we were
was a VHS tape
Fast Forward
Stop
Play

Stop
Rewind
Stop
Eject
Taken back to the store.
Long

OVERDUE

EVERYONE LEAVES YOU FOR DEAD IN THE END
FT. BF JONES

Answer the door,
Tie up your hair,
Let me in and let me speak.

Watch as the sludge
of swaying love-hate words
erupt from my whiskey lips

Sit on the mattress,
pull down the sheets,
let me in and let me be.

Listen to the arhythmic
beat of my too-many-times
patched-up heart

Open your mouth,
take off your clothes,
let me in and give me your breath

Feel the heat of the skin
I have draped over
my shattered bones

Lie down still,

close your eyes,
let me in and give me it all.

Close your eyes
and remember me as
I used to be.

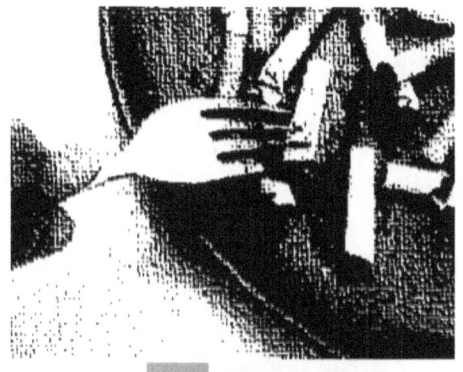

LEFTOVERS

The last one,
she left so much of herself behind
when she rode her bicycle away
from my apartment building that last time.

Sifting through the ashtray.
Picking through the bones of a half-eaten meal.
The soft fabric of dresses and lingerie
like flesh underneath my fingers, abandoned and
unclaimed.

This last one,
she took almost everything
when she left me, with the television on too loud,
sitting with an unlit cigarette in hand at a dining table set
for two.

That last one,
the final shred of evidence — a purple shower-sponge,
hanging like my bitter, little heart from a plastic hook in
the bathroom,
I'll never use again, but never really thrown away.

SMALLTOWN CRIMES

She hitched up the sleeve of her sweater. Momentarily.
I glimpsed all the cuts. Scabs. Hacking, jagged incisions.
Some still flowering with blossoms of dried blood.

I looked away.

A cry for help or just an itch that needed to be scratched.
More than any compassion for someone I should've loved,
I was pissed off she'd allowed me to become a witness
to her small-town crimes.

I had my own problems, after all.

We never discussed it then and she never let her mask slip again.
But so often, recollecting her that day,
it's like gazing into a cracked mirror and I'd like to
telephone her to talk about it all,
now she's made it out of all those clinics and hospitals.

I never will because perhaps she's as worried about double jeopardy as I am.

ALONE IN THE APARTMENT WITH A SILENCE CROUCHED LIKE A PIT BULL

Sitting on the sofa,
The television screen black,
As is everything else tonight.
Raining outside — I'm listening

to the sounds of a ventilator,
a respirator, raindrops
splashing, spreading, seeping, soaking
the tarmac, the concrete, and the glass.

None of it does any good.
The very walls scream absence.
She's in the place, skirting the raindrops,
and in the narrow passage between the silences.

Sometimes, I catch my reflection in the glass of
the riverbed windowpanes and wonder
why have I done this to myself again, and I contemplate
how long it'll take to bleed out fully

this time around?

"WHO DROVE YOU HOME LAST NIGHT?"
FT. DAVID CRANMER

A shadow cast by a butterfly in a bone jar.
A pillowcase net etched with lipstick marks of a stranger.
A cigarette half burned in an ashtray and a whiskey tumbler half empty.
These things I examine of a murder scene of you.

Death is a subtle sound
screaming to be heard.

It was a torrential fall. Hard and full on—drunk on regrets.
Words overflowed between us on the bed.
Did I pull the trigger or had you planned for some time to start anew?

OBLIGATED

My grandfather's body,
shriveled grey and mouth agonized agape.
In the morgue when I went to see him there.
Under lights humming too brightly of
finality and everything stinking of chemicals and of being
a day late,
a dollar short.
Dead wrong.
Just dead.

I never wanted to see *all that*.
What I wanted was to
remember him in life.
In full technicolor.
In constant motion.
With meaning.

But I was seventeen years old and obligated.
I told myself I was a man
And men should look upon death with
the same glancing indifference
they pass over the
changing of a green street signal.

But I was wrong then and
I am a man now
and I still often see that corpse,
shriveled grey and mouth agonized agape.
In the morgue when I went to see him there.

UNTITLED #444

The true suffering
of the poet is
knowing your death
will be noted,
your grave will be marked,
but your words will go
unknown and unrecognized.
Forever
and
ever
amen.

WHAT WE TALK ABOUT WHEN WE TALK ABOUT ANYTHING

Whenever you're at your happiest,
you seem to want to self-destruct.
You say
the worst possible things to those who
love you.
To drive them away. To make them
hate you.
Why?
I just can't understand it.

You burn every bridge and
then sit festering alone in your apartment,
drinking too much and not eating at all.
Talking about death
all the time.
Too much.
Why?
It's like you don't want to be happy.

Do you want to be happy?
You deserve happiness, you know that, right?
It's like you're addicted to it.
The misery.
Like you enjoy the pain of it all.

It doesn't help your writing. You think it does, but it doesn't.
Why do you kill everything you love?
I just can't understand it.
Have you thought about going back into therapy?

Well, say something.
Anything.
We can talk about anything you want.

HER NAME WAS JENNY

She lived across the street in a place called The Crescent.
Hollywood's ideal of what a twelve-year-old girl should be.
Four years older than I. She would always come over and play with my sisters, who were nearer her age,
in the summertime, when the days seemed to stretch out everlasting.
She had a sister my age. Sara, her name might've been.
She was always eating chocolate eclairs she wouldn't share and had these thick-framed glasses.
Sara wasn't allowed to play with us.
Jenny was always chewing cherry-cola bubble gum
and Jenny always wanted to play hide-and-seek.
When my sisters were counting, eyes closed, she would pull me across the yard, into the shed.
The shed was dark, cool, and smelled like wet wood.
Jenny would push me down on the floor and climb on top of me.
Push her mouth on mine.
Her tongue dancing around desperately.
Cherry-cola bubble gum filling my air passages.
I didn't know what she was doing, but I knew I liked it.
It got to the point I was pulling her into the shed and pushing her down.

One day, Jenny stopped coming over to play.

I waited in the front yard every afternoon as

that summer wound itself down to nothing.
I saw her with the gang of much older boys
who always hung around the old garages.

She was holding one of their hands. Pretended she didn't know me.
I don't know how I knew then, I was only eight years old,
but I knew,
I'd been something for Jenny to practice on. I remember sitting down

on the front step of my house with
a feeling like a block of slowly melting ice-cream in my guts.
It might've been the first bitter-sweet wound of many.

Finally, I gave up on Jenny,
stood up, dusted down my pants, walked over to Jenny's
house, and knocked on the door.
Her little sister Sara answered.
I asked her if she wanted to come over to my house and
play hide-and-seek.

FOR M + N II

I'd like very much to think,
one day after I'm dead and buried,
you'll be sorting through
your old man's things.
The junk I thought was important, that you'll look over quickly,
maybe grinning to yourself at some half-remembered nostalgia,
toss it in a black bag for the trash pile down the street.
Scraps of paper, old bills, creased tickets, luggage labels, and receipts.
Etcetera...
You've been told a lot about me. Your old man.
The good things, the bad, the ugly, the funny, the very disagreeable.
Some from your mother, some from me.
I want you to know I wasn't perfect, but I always tried my best.

I'd like very much to think,
one day, after I'm dead and buried,
you'll find this poem within this book, and know
I wanted to put it into immortal ink forever,

I am so very proud of you,
my girls,
and
I love you
so very much.

I haven't cried in front of another person since I was a kid.
I've cried alone in the empty smoking section of a coffee shop,
on a street at 4:30AM,
in a bathroom stall of a cancer ward,
but never in front of another person.

I hope I've met that person now,
who could watch me cry.
Release all those years' worth of stagnant waters,
and not really think about how it changes anything but the weather for a little while.
Wouldn't that be like being born again or baptized or atoned of all your sins.
To use those dirty waters to wash yourself clean.
Wouldn't that be something...

SOMETIMES

My muscles feel tired, head too heavy.
I'd like to just take a long train ride with you.

We'd be the only people in the whole carriage.
Our baggage tucked away cleanly beneath our feet.

Watching the waves and the rain crashing down outside
as we passed it all by, leaving it all behind.

Traveling softly together into a night
forever twilight and dark.

BREEZE

Add up all those words,
stack them up like so much firewood.
Those days, too, spent like dirty, creased cash
withdrawn from a savings account.

Ring-mark stains to be bleached.
Give those whispered words to the wind
with the dust and last autumn's leaves.
That's where they live now.

THE BEST ONES ARE THE CRAZY ONES

I've tried to love the good women.
The kind who talk about their day
with a vacant smile on their perfect lips,
who cook me delicious, healthy
dinners, and enjoy watching soap operas while
resting their head on my shoulder.
The women who answer questions frankly,
honestly, when I ask them.
Women who make me
feel content and confident.

But I always find myself going
back to the kind of women
who disappear some nights,
their phones switched off.
The type of women who will text me
the sexiest photographs when we're apart
and then send them to others
when I'm in the shower.
Or the women who lie about
what they ate for lunch,
who they met yesterday afternoon,
where they slept last night,
and the men who are calling
their cellphone while they are in bed, naked, with me.

The women who fake birth control or
are sleeping with me because

they're still angry with their ex-boyfriends
or their absent fathers.
The kinds of women who cheat with me and
then later cheat on me.

The ones I have to warn
that they're making a scene and
then they try to slap me, miss and
knock things that smash onto the floor.
Who run off into the night, threatening
to throw themselves off a bridge or
threatening to call the cops, or both.
Or worse.

The kinds of women,
I know, that'll see me swing from
the end of a rope one day and
smile a little.

I could say I love these kinds of women
because I just can't love myself.
Maybe there is
some truth in that,
but maybe it's just
they're a euphoric kind of self-harm
that I inflict on the ragged soul
instead of the flesh.

AN EPILOGUE

Used you up

like change in a payphone,

until I was only fighting with myself

down a deadline.

Thanks for reading! Find more transgressive fiction (poems, novels, anthologies) at: Outcast-Press.com

Twitter & Instagram: @OutcastPress

Facebook.com/OutcastPress1

GoFund.Me/074605e9 (Outcast-Press: Short Story Collection)

Amazon, Kindle, Target, Barnes & Nobel

Email proof of your review to OutcastPressSubmissions@gmail.com & we'll mail you a free bookmark!

20 dark short stories by debut and veteran subversive writers like Craig Clevenger, Greg Levin, Lauren Sapala, Stephen J. Golds, and more! Everything from serial killers and speculative cannibals to strippers and smack addicts.

MORE FROM OUTCAST PRESS

How would you feel if today was your last day on Earth? Lotus is the part of yourself you're afraid and ashamed by, all the bad thoughts you shove inside the darkest corner of your brain. This 18-poem literary/visual arts collection explores death, sex, drugs, drinking, honesty, and the after-life. With rock 'n' roll flare and an appreciation for nature, Austin Davis unravels everything from teenage degeneracy to the cosmos in under 50 pages.

ABOUT THE AUTHOR

Twitter: @SteveGone58   Site: StephenJgolds.WordPress.com

Stephen J. Golds was born in North London, U.K., but has lived in Japan for most of his adult life. As the co-editor of *Punk Noir Magazine*, he primarily writes noir and dirty realism. He enjoys spending time with his daughters, traveling the world, boxing, and listening to old soul LPs.

He is the author of 3 novels: *Say Goodbye When I'm Gone, I'll Pray When I'm Dying, Always the Dead*. He also has the poetry collections *Poems for Ghosts in Empty Tenement Windows* and *Love Like Bleeding Out with an Empty Gun in Your Hand*. His website is www.PunkNoirMagazine.com

www.ingramcontent.com/pod-product-compliance
Lightning Source LLC
Chambersburg PA
CBHW030044100526
44590CB00011B/321